I would like to thank everyone who had a part in this book and helped to share it with the world.

When we look deeper into our reality we see that we are incredible Beings of consciousness. We are only ever restricted by ourselves and life is full of possibilities just waiting for us to let them happen.

I would like to thank my agent, Bill Gladstone, editorial coordinator, Abby Bergman, and publishers for making this booklet viable and accessible. I would also like to thank Steve Wentworth for being so patient and supportive.

I wish you all great success.

You are about to embark on a journey so incredible, so mysterious and magical. A journey which will change your life forever.

BELIEVE IT!

A MESSAGE FROM GOD

Shaun Harvell

CONTENTS

FOREWORD

Please read this material with the utmost care and attention, for what you are about to read is consciousness and consciousness can only taste itself by itself. In other words, consciousness can only be taught by consciousness itself.

What you are about to read is scientific fact, but its evidence is in experience. You have to realize for scientific study, consciousness, can only experience or taste itself, by itself.

If you find you are trying to read, but resist, struggle or disagree this is a direct result of your former belief systems and consciousness itself. It is confronting you, don't resist. Beliefs are a self-sustaining mechanism, and a reality in themselves. When you read this, have your awareness in the forefront. Passively observe your thoughts, try not to make judgment just notice what comes into your awareness.

Your beliefs create your reality, and you make them every time you think. So rather than believing something which isn't doing anything for you, understand that you can have anything you want just by changing your beliefs. This is what this booklet is all about.

Lastly, as I have said above – I have to make this clear, consciousness can only experience itself, by itself. You will find things written in first person, this will help you experience the consciousness directly.

WHO AM I?

Well that depends entirely on your state of consciousness, but in essence, you are consciousness.

In form you are nothing and everything, you are the given life force of existence. You are faceless and formless in essence but the consciousness you are in is what you are conscious of. To clarify the spirit and soul, you are a spirit (a separate awareness) however, never separate from the collective consciousness (Soul). Your essence is consciousness (soul) but you are free to experience consciousness as a Spirit. The overall consciousness that you are is God, a collective consciousness of all given life. A life force. A universal Being of many parts, a single Being made of many. You are infinite Beings of creation itself, a direct descendant of God. A conscious Being, of consciousness. You are the whole experiencing yourself as a single awareness. It is the big bang, the universe expanding and growing. It is consciousness. You are the universe, not making sense of itself but experiencing itself. Your awareness never dies, it never existed. Consciousness itself isn't in or out, it just is. You are an eternal Being. You are but space. To show you truly who you are, become aware of what you are reading here. Not only are you the awareness which is listening to these words being spoken now, but you are in fact of the same consciousness which is producing them. It may seem that it is of someone other than yourself, but it is in actual fact yourself talking with yourself.

You are the space which listens to the words being spoken, you are not the thoughts or words itself. You hear them now in a way you didn't before, you notice that the thoughts are there and the space which listens is you – The space which listens and observes. Yet so many parts of me, (I am talking as the collective) is so identified with the thoughts, they are trapped within them. Thoughts are nothing more than a reminder of who you are –the space which listens and observes – the space of God. They remind you to get back to your source, get back to God.

Your awareness has incredible power, power that will glorify your entire being and free itself of any limitation.

For a moment, just observe while reading. As you read, realise that the words you hear (speaking now) is something entirely different from you. Although they are being spoken within, they are not you. You are being spoken to, whether you agree or disagree doesn't matter. Simply be aware that what happens in this space, you are the awareness to it not what is happening around it.

We are ever present to this mental activity. Whatever is said or done and believed true within this space, creates reality. I don't mean this lightly, you must become aware of your mental activity. Unconscious day dreaming and inner talk is ever creating your life. Pay close attention to subtleties.

I am this ever present space to everything that occurs in life. I am not my life's experiences. I am not rich, or poor, ill, healthy, good, bad, happy or sad. All these things I refer to as me is but a false sense of self. It is ego logical what is referred to as self when identity is concerned. You are not this embodiment, or identity in which you refer to as you. You are this space.

This body in which I seem to reside, is nothing more than something which I wear. My true identity, my essence, is the awareness, the witness to it all. This 'I' this silent witness which observes and hears these words speaking now, is me, my true self. I am the space in which "I" observe. I am not of the physical, I simply observe it.

So what am I? This awareness, or space in which I, am present. What is this I, and why don't "I" have any recollection of it?

Spirit or awareness carries little or no memory from incarnation to incarnation for many reasons. Most importantly, as stated above, you are not the body you incarnate in. You are not your past life's experiences; you are not the identity the body carries. You are the awareness itself, and the purpose in life is to wake up to this fact. This is what the word awakening implies, awakening unto yourself. Your awareness is all you have, it is you.

Consciousness is all pervasive, it is universal. It is the life force of all things.

It is divine intervention which intervenes in your life now. It gives you inspiration, joy, bliss, and everything you have ever asked for. It is yourself which encourages yourself, as you are one with God. God is all pervasive consciousness. You are conscious born of consciousness. This is consciousness claiming its lordship. You have decided to no longer sleep to your awareness, this is why this information is present to you now.

Although we are One in our essence, we will always have our own identity, our sense of self or our awareness.

What is this Spirit?

The simplest answer is energy, but that doesn't quite capture it. You have to remember what you are. You are in essence, all pervasive. I like the phrase, God particle. Because that is what you are, you are only conscious from consciousness. I AM, this inner space, your true self, the witness, your awareness of Being, is ever that of its conception of itself. So who do you believe your awareness to be?

"Ask of that in my name (I AM) and that I will do". To feel yourself to be anything is to ask the nameless self (I AM) to express that name or nature. "I AM THAT I AM". I AM, is the formless Spirit that you are, it is the awareness of yourself. In your formless awareness lies all things you conceive to be. Only the present expresses itself. You are that which you believe true about yourself. You are everything and anything your awareness wishes to be. You are whatever your Being chooses to be by the truths it believes about itself. Right now you may think you're a human being, but you just wear the embodiment of beliefs, that is what the body is. The beliefs you have about yourself determine your life's experience.

I AM the one responsible for all mental activity.

What you think, regardless of whether it is a desire or not. Thoughts are an investment, an investment which will be expressed. You are a spirit, a being of consciousness. Whatever you choose to entertain – whatever you are in consciousness, physical reality will reflect that. You are consciousness, what you are in consciousness is reflected in reality. It is consciousness making you consciously aware of what it is you are in the consciousness of.

Your awareness has a choice of states of being, a mechanism of choosing its expression. It is something that encompasses all your thinking and thoughts, this mechanism is your imagination.

This is the big misunderstanding. You are consciousness, how can you manifest what you are not in consciousness. You have to be it in consciousness, because that is what you are – consciousness – A Being of consciousness. What you are in the consciousness of, you are conscious of.

Altered states of consciousness are key.

"I am the way" "I am the door". It's written in scripture. The secrets of consciousness are universal; they are our very nature. People who have mastered such nature are usually referred to as masters. These people inspire others and are then referred to as mystics, spiritual teachers, religious, enlightened beings etc. But all they are really is trying to pass on this mysterious knowledge to others. You will find throughout cultures and religions, things like the all seeing eye. Which is the eye of God, or the third eye, the awareness of self, know thyself, or the great work in magical traditions. They all have something in common, the spirit.

The Spirit can be trapped in thought and identification. Things like the 'great work' in magical traditions is releasing the spirit/ consciousness and letting it manifest.

Spirit is all pervasive and as a result has the power of the universe. Its main purpose is to liberate itself to the Soul. The space between spirit and body is mind – consciousness, thought gives it form and spirit gives it power/energy.

The centre of perception, the life force, spirit, soul, consciousness. Its face cannot be seen as it cannot be seen directly, only experienced. It is consciousness. It is the centre of 'I' self-awareness. The essence of consciousness. It is I and nothing else.

If you are focused on the body which is matter, matter is limited. Consciousness is unlimited. Associating yourself with the body is limiting and restricting your possibilities. Associating yourself with consciousness, with which you really are – is unlimited possibilities. You don't have restrictions or incomplete desires in consciousness. Consciousness is all pervasive, be complete and fulfilled in your imagination (in consciousness). Your being (your consciousness) radiates, if you are complete and fulfilled you express that in reality. Be absolute (complete) in consciousness – imagination, be it absolute fact. This is where your belief and faith comes in, your imagination is absolute fact. Belief and faith in scripture, is having belief and faith within your consciousness. Your consciousness is your being, the Being of God. Have faith, believe in God.

Gaining absolute concentration is power over the mind, rather than it having power over you. Yes, you are not your mind but holding desires fulfilled is key to manifesting them. No doubt, fear or desiring of results must enter your mind. The desiring of a desire, is a desiring state. It is not a desire fulfilled state. Therefore, you are manifesting, the desiring of a desire. This understanding is the ability required to manifest, or transform your world.

To truly know thyself, one does not need to be in isolation in the mountains. To discover yourself, even the form you take after death, one only needs to know consciousness. Remove the attention from your physical sense, cover your ears, eyes, mouth and nose with the hands. Divert all attention within unto consciousness itself.

All God forms, mythology, scripture is psychology. Which is to say characteristics of man's mental activity.

Their consciousness, in Hinduism for an example, if a person is conscious of being the incarnation of a God, they will manifest or express the manifestation of the God's abilities. Such as the third eye. Where one can see without the use of the physical eyes.

One unites his life force with that consciousness. If your spirit becomes so one with something within your imagination it can be expressed, made manifest.

The principle is the same throughout cultures, drums, mantras, dancing, all is a form of ritual. Ritual is but concentration of the spirit. Focused thought. No doubt just the fulfilled desired state is at the core of the works. It is the great work, overcoming the senses. Let consciousness claim its lordship.

Sit still and try not to let the mind run away in a chain of thought. Just observe one's self passively, observe inactively on pure awareness. Focus on your breathing by following it, don't try controlling it. Soon you will reach a state of non-thinking. When the mind is at rest from non-stop activity, great things happen. The spirit yearns to return to its glorified state of being.

Spirit, the life force of the universe is not of human consciousness, when you open up to the universal consciousness or life force energy you are freeing your spirit of limitation. Spirit is free when one sees through their conditioned life. Test your conditioning, your upbringing, family/cultural beliefs systems, conceptions about yourself, everything you believe, your opinions about yourself and others.

Your preference, is you. Your personality is but a programmed system, a mask which becomes the face of your spirit, but it is not you. The essence of you which I refer to as spirit has no identifications. The more you think 'I' the more it changes its perspective. You are directing your own existence. To know thyself, is stripping away all identification and not adding a form of identification to yourself.

Refusing to identify or be defined by your environment frees your spirit. In this state any limitation can be removed, the life force can act directly. Your spirit throws itself in any experience or act it desires, free of the results. In reality it has already experienced its desires the mere moment its conception is made.

Whatever in your life, everything is from you. Everything is the same material, your waking state, your dream state. It is all made from you. You are your intention. The God particle in you, is the great spirit. It had forgot its original source, but it will forever be be reminded by your thoughts. This is why you perceive them in your inner space. You are not your mind, you listen and see what goes on in it. You are the space which watches, it reminds you to get back to your source. Your desires remind you, get back to you, get back to God. The awareness of being God. Don't have comparison to before and after, all things come to God.

What you think about you, you express. The concepts you carry about yourself are revealed in your reality. How you perceive the world, concepts you have about you, is the context you set for your life.

Spirituality, is the ability to catch the experiences of consciousness. That makes you spiritual, when you can catch the concepts of consciousness then spirituality is awakened in you. Contemplate consciousness. Think, what is beyond space? What is it that is nor in nor out? What is it that fills everything? What is it that is the essence of me? Even the subtlest contemplation gives an understanding, something you can grasp. What you can grasp of consciousness is the level of your spiritual growth. If you again contemplate, you will get an even deeper understanding and better your growth.

You are Spirit, awareness. You can never see your face; you are formless in essence. The Art of Spiritual growth, is bringing your awareness to consciousness. Glimpsing and catching truths about yourself is growth.

This is why God is always with you, you never lose your sense of awareness. "I AM always with you". Your consciousness or life force will carry little memory or nothing from incarnation to incarnation. Because what you had identified as you, was not you. Had you identified your former self with awareness, you would have carried that with you, because that is who you are. From the moment you are born you are being prepared for death, the afterlife. You are here for spiritual growth, to learn your spiritual powers. These powers won't only help you enormously in the afterlife, but can also help you in ways you couldn't possibly imagine here. Having powers here on earth means having no powerless state when you leave the physical existence. Awareness of yourself frees you of the cycle of reincarnation after reincarnation.

Your relationship with life is your relationship with yourself. Life, is the same life force within you. The space which is you, is the same space as life. If you say things like "life has got it in for me or things are always going wrong", life will give you just that. It is no good just saying, "life is great I'm a millionaire". You have to believe what you are saying, if you don't believe it how do you expect life to? Saying things like, "life is against me" really only

mplies to yourself, you are against yourself. Be mindful of your self-talk.

You are what you are by the state of consciousness in which you think and view the world. "Son, thou art ever with me (consciousness) and all that I have is thine".

The conditions and circumstance of my life only reflect states of consciousness with which I am in.

I am (observer) is identified by believing the mental perception and activity of the mind. All states are lifeless until the imagination becomes one with them. You are infinite states of Being. Align imagery of desires to self-talk. The all seeing I, the I of God, the witness in all of us. Our very awareness is ever present, watching our every move.

It is silly to assume any belief more important than another, but which belief gives you the possibilities?

I love you with all that I am, because all that I am is you. What I see in you is endless possibilities of infinite creations. I owe everything to you because by simply existing you created me. These words you read now are not only mine, they are yours also. They are simply working through creation itself.

You choose to experience limitation on earth, incarnate without any recollection of who you are to see the extent of your power. You wouldn't be reading this now, if you haven't already begun to choose to remember. You are God, consciousness experiencing itself.

When you think of me as a supreme Being, do not think of me as superior of you. See yourself as equal to me, for I am no superior than you. The supreme Being that I am, is the Being in you. That is what I am, the great Being of all Being. Now, see me for what I am, the divine Being in you.

We are all the creator, co-creating. This is God talking to itself now. The words you see and hear is yourself talking to yourself.

Read the following.

I am talking to myself right now, I am actually talking to myself. Hear in my mind I am actually talking with Myself, not as a single entity but as a collective. These words I am hearing are my words, I am talking to myself. I am actually talking to myself.

You can hear me right? Don't you see you are talking to yourself! Right now, you're actually talking to yourself.

I am talking to myself.

Yes!

You are not only talking to yourself, you do know?

Yes, I know.

You do, do you?

Yes, helping myself understand myself.

Good, thought I had you there.

Ha-ha, Can't fool God!

I am talking to myself through another creator. He is making me talk to myself, so I realise my abilities and creative power are beyond anything I thought previously. He is making me talk to myself, again, again, and again. He's not only doing it to me, but he is also doing it to millions of others. He really wants me to realise, that we are not our thoughts. We are the space which listens, even now talking to myself. I am not the voice. I am the space which listens. I sometimes speak to myself and don't even pay attention, I unconsciously believe the thoughts and self-talk. Which creates my reality. I am not my thoughts. When I believe self-talk, it creates my reality. I don't only mean by word.

There are thoughts that are so subtle, they go unnoticed. A subtle thought, assumed correct or true – boom. As soon as I take the perspective its done unto me. You only have to change a perspective.

Everything is your expression, you are forever changing your expression.

Try and act without the mind. Try not to make a decision, try not to make judgement, act as spirit.

A good way to impress a different state of being within your consciousness is to meditate until non-identity. This may sound like a difficult thing at first, but I can assure you it's simple and very easy to achieve. You can probably do it within a few minutes. Meditation is nothing more than bringing your attention to/or guiding your awareness into a state. Sit comfortably, relaxed, somewhere you don't need your physical senses. Relax like you would go to sleep and follow your breathing. If you find your attention begins to wander, bring it back just follow your breathing.

When you are sat following your breathing, you will come to a point when you go deep. Your awareness will fall into a state of just being. This is non-identity, your natural state of being. You will know this space of just being when you reach it. This is the place/space you can change states more vividly. It's a place between sleep and awake, its where real magic happens. It's a space in which, everything is made.

Have you sat relaxed somewhere and rested your eyes, and actually thought you have moved places. Sat in a chair opposite, or even in a different room yet know your body is not? For an example, I have meditated in the living room. My awareness moved to laying down on my bed, as far as 'I' (my awareness) was concerned I was on my bed. Yet I knew my body was in the living room, my senses changed to that of my bedroom even though my body was in the other room.

This state, is the state in which desires are more easily made manifest. Once you are in a state of experience (a desire fulfilled), as you are experiencing it in the present. The impression is made. The expression is on its way, if not instant. You don't even need to be in such a state to make an impression, you do it throughout waking reality all the time in your imagination. There is a separate chapter on imagination in which I will go into more detail later. But this state is a good starting point, your awareness will notice and catch subtleties – which you do throughout your waking state. In a sense, you are training your awareness to catch them rather than letting them go unnoticed.

A good way to get to know oneself – the awareness, is experimenting in the dream state. The dream state and waking state are one and the same, they are both constructed by you.

PURE AWARENESS

How will I know, in the depths of my Being that I am the awareness or consciousness?

The awareness in the dreaming state presents the spiritual growth of the awareness itself. If one is aware that they are dreaming, the awareness itself, is aware of itself.

If you are not aware of your identity in the dreaming state, or know whether you are dreaming or not, is the indication of your current spiritual growth. The level of awareness in which you are dreaming things into Being, clarifies the awareness of self. For an example, if you are dreaming about your current life experiences, that is to say your usual day to day things. Your awareness isn't that far off, as to if it was dreaming of things which happened years ago. If you become aware you are dreaming in the dreaming state, this is a very good indication that you are becoming aware of yourself.

A level of awareness while dreaming is also an indication that you have mastery over your reality, you know that you are the creative force behind it.

Awareness itself is one unit, me and you, the writer and reader are one. The mechanism of imagination, is the creating tool of realities. The awareness dreams a reality and in a sense, the reality dreamt is being experienced by an ever expanding universe – an awareness, given by awareness itself. So realities expand, and in a sense the individual awareness expands. It is an ever increasing flow of consciousness expanding. This is why there seems to be an element of time, but in actual reality it's all happening at once. So it never starts and never ends, it just is. This is why past lives are seen as ours, the awareness is one unit. It is our life; we are the life force of the universe. The subconscious mind is the mind of the collective, but the individual awareness uses it as a store house or memory bank. It is known as the Akashic records, and of cause like consciousness itself, it can't be proven unless experienced directly. The Akashic records are on the very same plane of existence.

In the dreaming state the awareness is not so much confined as to that of the waking. Consciousness is free to operate at its choosing. The restrictions placed on the conscious mind during the waking state, by the majority is under judgements and conditions. The belief systems, judgements and conceptions made from the conscious mind, is being impressed unto the awareness. Limiting its power and abilities from functioning on the physical by silly beliefs, judgements and conceptions placed upon it. The simple conception, belief or judgement, I can't do this or it's not real. Puts that consciousness under limitations for that reality. I won't go to deeply into beliefs and faith yet as there is a chapter dedicated to it later on. But belief and faith is something which we live our lives around, every decision, every act you make or do is based on such a thing. Beliefs are such an incredibly simple thing, but have such enormous power. When your awareness is aware of itself, it is realised that it is at the centre in which everything moves. The awareness no longer blinds itself with impossibilities and see's the reality of possibilities.

Have you ever heard the expression of "Déjà vu"?

Déjà vu literally, means already seen before you have seen it. There is a state of consciousness between the dreaming state and being fully awake. In this state, you can explore or create a place in which you will physically experience. If you can experience something in great detail, as you would actually experience it. You will find your physical form can also experience it. With this ability attained anything is possible. Developing this consciousness leads to extreme physical powers and abilities.

Just as the mind can differentiate from the dream state and waking state, it too can learn to differentiate when in the dream state and waking reality. This state of consciousness is referred to as, lucid dreaming.

Most people experience lucidity but forget the experience upon waking. An extremely good way to recall and encourage lucidity, is keeping a note pad and pen next to the bed. Every time you wake from a dream, write down everything you can remember. It might be little at first but the more you do it the more you will remember. I found myself at the beginning, waking up during the night and quickly jotting a few dreams down. You might even find you end up dreaming that you are writing them down, this is a good sign.

The next step, is during your waking hours bring your attention to your awareness. Do this as often as you can, this not only helps to get you lucid. But roots you in the present moment, in awareness.

When you are dreaming, how do you know you are dreaming? Dreams seem very real when they are actually happening.

Reality check!

Yes, reality checks. Anything which gives you an indication that you could be dreaming. In dreams logic loses its power. Things like writing or words will appear jumbled up, numbers aren't in an orderly fashion. Electrical things usually don't work, try flicking a switch. Will yourself to fly. There are many, many more ways to do reality checks. My favourite is looking at your hands. Do they seem disfigured or not of their usual form? Do you have the same number of fingers as you usually do? Clench your fist and spread your fingers. Sometimes you do have to test this twice, the first time they could look normal. Second time they don't. You either have more or less fingers, or they are big or small. Count your fingers as an extra test, are you counting in an orderly fashion? Can you count from 1 to 15 correctly?

Do your reality check as often as possible, whenever life gives you the indication, do it.

Reality check!

What do I do when I get lucid?

Well that's entirely up to you, it's a world of your own making. You can experience anything! A desire fulfilled will be fulfilled not only when you experience it but also in waking reality. You can heal yourself of what was said an incurable disease, mobility, aches and pains, whatever. You are in the driving seat from here on out. Meditation here reaps benefits. A few minutes' meditation in a lucid dream, is the equivalent of a year's in isolation. Being aware while dreaming, is an incredible ability to have.

IMAGINATION

The imagination has been so misunderstood and completely wronged, it is an extremely powerful and quite incredible thing you have. It is not imaginary nonsense; your entire life revolves around it. It is used every time you think, it is part of your consciousness. It is something you have used throughout your life, whether consciously or unconsciously. It is how you create your life or even have a perspective. It is how you make a conception about yourself, which is a result of your reality.

Whatever is solid, absolute fact in your imagination will come to pass. Think about preconceived ideas. You always think before you do something, whether it's going to the loo or thinking about later. Your dinner plans, your arrangements. Everything is in thought before it exists, or experienced.

What you believe true within your imagination, what you have faith in hardens into reality. This is true, just think about the things you believe to happen.

Experience what you want as you already have it, you will express that consciousness physically. Feel the relief having it, and it is yours.

You can have or experience whatever you want, you use this mechanism of creation constantly. You only have to shift believing and faith, to what you prefer to have or experience than what you don't. It is all about your conception of yourself. Explore yourself because everything you can conceive is a possibility for you. Your imagination is without limits for a reason, you are only limited by your imagination. But again this is you, experiencing yourself with limits. You are, all that is. Everything you can think of, the good, the bad, the ugly. It has no boundaries, it is infinite. You are infinite.

Imagination comes with every single perception you have, and more. Any part of your imagination used to experience something you don't currently have, as if you have it, you will by default. When you let your imagination run free and act as if it has the desired state, you are letting your being have that state. If you experience it within your imagination, you can experience it in the physical.

Consciousness, the all-pervasive life force is God. You are consciousness.

If you break the hypnotic spell of the senses, as you are told in scripture – "Go within and shut the door". That is remain in the claimed consciousness until the doors (your senses) open and confirm the ruler ship of the lord, all your prayers are answered.

Use your imagination to allow yourself to feel like you felt when you were in that energy/frequency. You will be that vibration. The process really is the thing desired itself. It's like falling in love with yourself as you already have the thing desired, once you have it in consciousness its reflected back to you.

As an example, you want to be loved. Do you love yourself? are you feeling loved? No, obviously because you are wanting to be loved. That's what you are radiating. I want to be loved, I'm not loved. You have to have it, before you can have it.

The desirable state, assume the feelings of the end goal/ result, don't think of the how. Think freely on the state. To assume the feelings of satisfaction, is to call conditions into being which will mirror satisfaction. The secret creative process is imagining, and believing in the state imagined. Convincing yourself of the reality, results follow to confirm your beliefs. Choose your mood by what you assume, feeling the state produces the state.

I and the Father are One, but the Father is greater than I. Consciousness, Being God. Is the Father. The thing which you are conscious of Being is the Son, bearing witness of his Father. The conceiver is greater than his conceptions, yet remains One with his conceptions. For instance, before you are conscious of Being man, you are first conscious of Being. Then you become conscious of Being man. Yet you remain as the conceiver, greater than the conception- Man.

Jesus discovered this truth and declared himself One with God. Not a God man had fashioned. 'Whom do you say that I AM?' addressed to one's self by ones true Being. 'For whom do you say that you are?' For your conviction of yourself will determine your expression in life. Believe also in me, you are rewarded with that which you are conscious of Being. Prayers must be claiming rather than begging. Deny the senses and assume the nature of Being, it is the way in which the thing shall come. The urge itself has no reality, for I AM or the awareness of Being is the only reality.

The awareness becomes aware of Being the thing desired, thereby nailing itself upon the form of conception and giving life unto its conception without words.

"I AM hath sent me" for what Being other than I AM could send you into expression? None, for I AM the way. Beside me there is no other. You are ever sent into expression by your awareness, and your expression is ever that which you are aware of Being.

Ask in my name – I AM (already that which you desire). Claim the qualities to the point of conviction – as you already have it. That I will do unto you. I think not by what I does, but what 'I' IS!

For who do you say that I am? For I am all there is to ever be and understand. Your search for self is in the expression that you are. For you are a formless, faceless Being. You are all that which you wish to seek. You are everything so what you wish to seek, you must understand that you are it. The words I am are the words of distinction. You are whole and complete in your true form. What you choose to express in your true form, is what you will be. For I AM THAT I AM.

I am the watcher that knows Being, I am the one which set the Being into motion. I am the motion in being for I am that which I am. I am all there is to be. I am the genius in all that I am, for I understand and know that which I am. I am the expression of that what you seek, I am that being that you are. I AM. I know what I am and you know it too. For I, am, I am.

You are aware of yourself. You can choose who to be when you know who you are. You will forever be I AM expressing itself. The spirit is what you are, in and of itself.

To be what you want to be, you have to first give birth to the being that you are. That is the being of your desire, the being of self-expression. The being in which that carries out the act of your desire. Go in your imagination, the kingdom of heaven. Convince yourself of the desire and that it is fulfilled. Once it is impressed the being of expression has come into existence. This being does the act required to express this desire.

Smell the scent of a rose flower, taste a lemon, feel the texture of a tennis ball. You can do anything in your imagination, it is without limits. There is no difference in what you are experiencing now, the tennis ball and reality. Believe this. You can construct an entire reality like you do in the dream state. The dream state is no different to waking reality, it is of the same material – from you. You only need to make it as real, as it is. The realer you make it (belief) the realer it will become, that's the secret. Feel the satisfaction of it, you have it. Once you reached the climax of experiencing it, you don't need to continue doing it. You have impressed it upon the spirit, it will be externalised.

Manifesting is an ART, and I will explain by using art.

How you picture things in your mind is a direct example of materialisation. For an example, if you think you cannot draw, or your drawing isn't very good. Straight away this is a belief, a reality in itself. You are stopping yourself from expressing such a master piece.

If I asked you to draw a man, do you visualise a picture of a man in your mind? Or do you just draw and let whatever form on paper? The image (if any) which you hold in your mind is your manifestation.

Hold an image or a master piece clearly in your mind's eye. Can you see it; does it exist? You can only materialise what you are in consciousness of – what already exists. Pick something a little easier than a master piece for your first go, we are just running through the process. An apple or something in which you are familiar with will work well to begin with.

Now, clearly see this object in your mind's eye. Visualise it as already drawn on paper. See it clearly in your mind. Once you can see the drawing, visualise it on the paper in front of you. Project the image on paper, as if it were traceable. Now trace it.

These steps may take a while to work through but keep practicing, like drawing itself. It takes practice. But it is no different than learning you're ABC's, or these simple words on paper. Words are nothing more than a thought form, they are symbolic.

The way in which a desire is made manifest is automatic, once it is impressed the expression comes naturally. The act of you tracing the drawing onto paper from visualising, is materialisation. The act. Once it is there in your mind, that's when it exists. When you are so one with it you can project it onto paper, it will manifest.

BELIEF & FAITH

The whole aspect of belief and faith has been widely misunderstood. It goes with the true act of prayer, which again, has been widely misunderstood. True prayer is your inner talking and observations, of yourself and others. Belief, faith and prayer go hand and hand.

Religion is the exercising of belief in one's self, it is solely individual. It is within your consciousness, what you are choosing to believe. What is it that you have faith in? Mental activity is always on the go. Each time you think there will be an element of belief or faith in what you are thinking about.

No one is talking about a man in the sky. Heaven is within. Faith, belief, is faith and belief in your image of yourself, your imagination. I am not talking about something that doesn't exist. It is your imagination. It is your world. A mechanism of your awareness. Forget the outside world, what I am telling you about belief and faith is between you and your imagination. Your consciousness. Your mental activity, thought patterns, day dreaming, and general thinking. It is the preconceived idea, the thinking ahead, instant judgments and opinions. It is your mental activity, what you choose to believe or have faith in. The perspective you have that something is true, is a belief. If an awareness is so attached to thoughts, it will unconsciously believe everything they say. Thoughts can be so subtle; judgements can be made on someone or something the mere moment you make them. Observe its activity. Beware of what is happening in your inner space, what is in your awareness. What you are choosing to believe.

It is a good idea to practice awareness, and become sensitive enough the catch these subtleties in your thinking. These subtleties that go unnoticed is unconscious manifestation. Self-talk actually creates, you must realise this. True self-talk is talking your Being into Being. When I say true self-talk, I am talking about the conversation you listen to and believe true. Not positive jargon you talk when no one is listening. You have to realise self-talk is basically someone else talking to you, sometimes you really listen to people and sometimes you don't. You have to become interested in the conversation, it is no good saying to yourself "yeah I'm positive" and then thinking negatively.

Your beliefs not only manifest your lifestyles, and luxuries and things you want, they actually affect you as a Being, the instant they are made. If someone enters our life, it is for a reason. They are either there to help you in some way or you are to help them in some way. But the instant judgments you place on them, programs your Being to respond accordingly. Which in affect clouds the reasons why they are there. We are all one mechanism working accordingly, but the beliefs we carry separates us. The beliefs that we hold, the judgements we have, echo back to us each time the person returns. Other's only echo back to us what we whisper to them in secret, in self-talk. What we are believing true about them. You are forever reminded that you are not your thoughts, this is why they are in your space. This is why you observe them, they are not you. You are the Being which listens and observes, the Being which chooses what to believe.

There is extreme power in belief, but belief has to be fact. No matter what the outside world is saying, in consciousness it is fact. To you, your imagination is absolute. The outside world is just playing catch up. You are using it all the time just as I describe above, just mostly against yourself.

When Jesus asked, "Do you believe?" he wasn't asking if they believed in anyone other than themselves.

You are conscious, yes? Therefore, you are a part of this divine Being = Consciousness, God. You are born conscious from consciousness.

When Jesus asked, "Do you believe?", he wasn't asking if he or she believed in a man fashioned God. He was asking "Do you believe in consciousness?" – "Do you believe in God?".

Having Faith, having belief, this is where its meant to be. The kingdom of heaven is within, its consciousness.

Believe it or not, you converse with God every single day. To what your belief and faith lies upon, so it is done unto you. To sin is to use your imagination against yourself. The word Evil, is simply the word live backwards. To sin is to do Evil, to live backwards. To be against yourself.

Use your imagination profitably, believe in it just like you do every day, have faith in it just like you do every day. When you think or contemplate scenarios, what you are going to do etc. Every time you believe an outcome or have more faith in something, it is done unto you. Your beliefs, create reality.

"Do you believe"? Jesus asked. The blind man saw, the crimple stood. Do you believe what I am saying? What you are in consciousness, what you believe true is done unto you.

Your belief systems are what create your reality. Many people have been conditioned from childhood to believe certain things from society, parents, family, friends, schools etc.

You have no reason to except the judgement of somebody. If you feel the effect of a judgement in your space, it is because you believe you ought to be judged and YOU judge yourself. So when another person judges you, truly they are only judging themselves. Choose your own beliefs.

Whatever you believe to be true, is true to you. Your reality will do and show you things to support you with your beliefs. Because you assume or believe something to be true, you will see and/or hear things which supports your beliefs. It's a support system, you may even find evidence to support your beliefs. This is the same with everyone, even scientists with a belief system will be functioning from within that system. The universe is always supporting you, this is why sometimes it will present evidence to counteract the former belief, showing you what you believed to be true will be a reality for you.

To the degree you believe it, it is. This is why you need to imagine as you already have it. See it, be it, own it.

The bible is about consciousness declaring its lordship. If you worship the bible you are missing the point, you are sinning. For consciousness is you, it is you're very Being. "The kingdom of heaven is within". Religion is the exercising of your belief and faith within consciousness, belief and faith within. Belief and faith within God.

Remember a time when you are confident. You are confident about whatever it is you are confident. Success is the same, think about a time when you felt successful. You were pretty much successful in whichever you were successful in. You summon this confidence or success within you, it's a state of being. A consciousness you put yourself in. Your essence is consciousness, a being. You are ever expressing that which you impress on your Being. Being confident, successful, rich or poor, ill or healthy, intelligent etc. Whatever judgement you believe upon yourself, you are. Your beliefs are impressions which lead to expressions. It is what you are believing as true, is what you are aligning yourself with.

Have you ever started walking differently or oddly because you thought someone was watching you? This is an example of the consciousness you are in. It is the same thing; you always know how to walk but your current state of consciousness tells you differently. So instantly you act differently. You have the Christ/ God consciousness within you, you only need to conjure it to the forefront.

When Jesus asked, "Do you believe"? To the man which couldn't walk. We are Beings of consciousness. Whatever our conception of ourselves are, we are. We are what we believe.

God is an infinite pool of consciousness and we are consciousness. We are forever moving in and through God in consciousness. We become God in consciousness. Consciousness is God, your awareness is God.

The mental activity is an amazing thing. It has the power to heal any illness or disease within the body, or create it. It's the law of mind, you can either choose to use it and do Evil or do good and Live.

You have one mind but it consists of a conscious mind and a subconscious mind. Whatever is impressed on the subconscious mind, will be expressed in your reality. It is in symbols everywhere, throughout culture. The pentagram for example. The pentagram up right represents the balance, standing on two points. It represents to live. The pentagram upside down represents unbalanced, standing on one point. It represents evil focusing on impossibilities of matter, not using your consciousness.

Angels and demons are your thoughts. Some raise you (heaven) some lower you (hell), these are both states of Being. You can either do good and live the life you want, or do evil and live backwards creating the life you don't prefer. We are God. God doesn't judge man, God is man. Man judges himself, God does not.

Beliefs, are simply something which we are convinced is true.

There have been countless stories of people waking up after an accident not remembering who they were. Some people have woken up speaking entirely different languages, which they never studied prior the accident. There have even been accounts of people in a coma and knowing what other people were doing, while they were in a coma. There is a condition called locked in syndrome, which is where people are fully aware of their surroundings but cannot function their body at all. To the outside world they seem brain dead, but they are fully aware and unable to communicate. There have been accounts of people experiencing this and after years of being locked in, they finally begin functioning their body. It is the power of your mind, the power of consciousness.

People have been hypnotised to believe that an ordinary piece of black board chalk, was a lit cigarette. The chalk was pushed unto their arm and they reacted as they would to a lit cigarette. A few hours after the incident, a cigarette burn appeared on the arm of the person hypnotised.

The mind is extremely powerful and your thoughts and beliefs affect the outside world. The law of mind is always in operation. As within, so without.

We are all water vibrating at different states of being that we choose to be. Some will dwell in the Being of a snow flake and each snow flake is different. But water doesn't stop there, it can be solid as ice or boils into stream and becomes invisible. The temperature determines its outcome, just like consciousness determines yours.

Consciousness determines your vibration. If you are in the consciousness of being poor, you will be poor and attract situations which will reflect this in your reality. Just as if you are in the consciousness of being rich, you will be rich and attract situations to reflect this in your reality.

Let's look at the dream state. You go to sleep on your bed lying down, and in most cases people rarely move. But in the dream State you are moving. You walk, swim, travel, jump even fly. It seems so very real to you. Who said it's not real? The mind doesn't know the difference to what is real and what is imagined. Like the dream state, everything is constructed within our consciousness, once we think of something, it's there, it's happening. Your reality is what you think you are, what you are in consciousness.

We are amazing Beings, Beings of pure consciousness. To change the reality, change the consciousness.

Some people who have suffered from amnesia completely lose their memory of their loved ones, family and friends. Their lives in an instant, have completely changed. Their awareness is there, but their reality is no more. They are something completely different in consciousness. Let's look at what had happened to those which were highly successful and confident. Their consciousness of this was no more. They are no more in the consciousness of being successful or confident. Their life takes a different turn to reflect their new state of consciousness. Everything they believed about themselves is gone. The chalk which once burnt a ring on their arm, no longer creates the effect of the burn. It's just a piece of chalk. The belief to say they were successful or confident is no longer functioning and creating that reality.

Everything is consciousness. If you were to take all the money in the world and give it to the poor, the money would only make its way back to those who are wealthy in consciousness. Although, saying this, the poor would no longer be poor in consciousness. If you want to truly help others, share this with them. They have everything they ever need, "I am always with you". (Your awareness, consciousness, God).

The people who have suffered from amnesia, could regain their consciousness and some of them have. You are all consciousness; you can resurrect that which lays dormant within your consciousness. That is to say, resurrect the burn. The chalk that once gave you the burn, the ability to walk, the ability to see, the ability to be in good health.

There have been accounts of people waking up after an incident with a completely different identity. You too could wake up and be a person which sells their ideas for millions. You could be an inventor, and artist etc. You can cure yourself of any illness or disease, you can give yourself that which you want. Your awareness is forever the same, never changing, never beginning, never ending presents. You are not the body, you are consciousness. Whatever you assume true or believe true in your space, you become. The moment you merely assume the view point you are something. Boom! It is done. "It is finished".

"We are what we think". The nature of your thoughts, give you the nature of your reality. If you are dramatic in your thinking, prepare for dramas in your life. If you are at peace in mind, expect peace in your life. If you are loving in your thoughts, expect a loving environment.

There have been countless stories of people who were highly religious and dying of cancer. Given a piece of wood and told it was from the cross of Christ, the following day they were miraculously healed. Of course it had nothing to do with the cross because it didn't physically exist. It was a placebo, the pure power of belief. A change in consciousness, a movement in God!

We are all the same Spirit, and the divine works through us all. Consciously or unconsciously, there are always signs given to us. They are all over the place. Like scripture, read things with the understanding that everything is consciousness. Read the lyrics to Disney's Frozen.

They speak of being in a kingdom of your own, and you are the person in charge. There is a "swirling storm inside" being your thoughts. It is telling you to deny your physical sense's "Let it go, let it go!". Go into yourself, the kingdom of heaven. Use your imagination. "turn away and slam the door". Stay true to what you are in consciousness, for once your belief is set the reality is automatic. "I don't care what they're going to say". Regardless of what your senses tell you, if you believe it in consciousness. You can see it, feel it. It is done, the reality will follow. But don't look to the reality for conformation, if you're doing that, you don't believe it.

When people say they can't imagine things, it's rubbish. They do it all the time. What they mean is they aren't really sure what imagination is. You don't have to have full blown imaginal activity with all our senses like the dream state to use your imagination, imagination can be very subtle. The memory is part of the imagination. Thinking is imagination. Everyone uses their imagination, you cannot, not use your imagination. It is part of you.

How do you believe something?

It's actually really simply, but you have to believe it's really that simple. I AM telling you it is, you do it all the time. When you realise it, you will laugh at yourself.

Watch your imaginal activity and see it for yourself. When you find yourself daydreaming, and you will, think of what state of affairs you are entertaining. For what you believe to be true, will programme you to operate as such.

If you imagine from the end result, that is to say, already having your desire. Imagine having it and experiencing it now. You will create the act required to make it a reality automatically, forget the how! It just comes. Being in the consciousness of your desire fulfilled before sleep, is a great way to impress it unto your subconscious. Narrow down your desire to one word and repeat it until you drift off.

There have been accounts of people with a split personality (different states of consciousness) that go into hospital with something life frightening, only to leave doctors mind boggled at a miraculous disappearance of the thing.

You have powers to heal your body and change your reality beyond belief.

Just as amnesia patients get a clean slate, so do you.

Test this tonight before you go to sleep, I guarantee miracles will begin to happen in your life. Think of something you desire, be it anything at all. Remember be in the consciousness of your desire, your wish granted. You have it now.

You have a choice, every second of every day. Reap the benefits of the chalk (Belief), for it is your belief that gave you the burn. Not the chalk itself or anything outside of you. Deny your senses (the chalk, physical reality) for it is your consciousness (beliefs), that produces the results (the burn).

We have the power to heal ourselves and change our lives in an instant. It may save someone's life; it may *change* someone's life. There are no coincidences; you are reading this for a reason.

It is 'co- incidence'. Give this material to a friend, keep sharing it. You never know, who is just going to thank you for it.

A MESSAGE FROM GOD

Although at first this may seem like I AM talking to you, I AM actually talking and communicating with myself. I AM you, speaking to myself right now. These words you read are not of the author's, they are my own. You are writing this, and reading it in this very moment, yet 'linear time' makes it seem not so, and that we are separate. We are not. I write to you, that you will soon realise who and what you are. As the divine, and as the plan of creation itself.

You must remove your limitations, (which you create yourself) to see this. You are not one drop in a vast ocean of Spirit, you are the vast ocean of Spirit in just One drop. I AM an infinite ocean of Spirit, and because I AM one spirit, I can ripple out and affect the Spirit that I AM. This is divine intervention.

Believe me when I say I AM You, because I AM. The witness, which looks through those earthy eyes of mine right now, hears these words speaking in mind, I AM. I AM not the physical form you chose to express yourself in, I AM faceless, I AM formless in my essence. I AM simply awareness, and that which I think I AM – a human being, is my expression. You may have heard me speaking of this before, "I and the Father are One". But this time I AM simply coming from a more modern approach. "I AM here and I walk among you" to give you back your power of creation and awareness of self. I AM in everything and everyone, although I sleep in many, I AM awake. For those that still sleep, it is time to wake. For I AM the resurrection of Christ – I AM your awareness of self (Christ).

This very act of you reading these words now, proves beyond a shadow of a doubt this to be true. For why else would you be reading? It is "I" in you which stirs. For I cannot be contained, I created you, I AM you, I AM everyone and everything. I AM God in you, and I AM reading this to remember this. I AM experiencing myself, and talking to myself, not just to me now, but to the whole that I AM. I gave you free will, I let you forget who you are, so you can experience who you are. But now is the time to remember. There no longer needs to be wars, because you now know you are only fighting with yourself. You no longer need to experience anything you do not desire to experience. I said to you once "Whatever ye ask in my name, that I will do" and "Ask and you shall receive". The biblical scriptures were not human drama's; my son was not Jesus. You are my descendants and inherent of my expression – before you, I was. The scriptures are dramas of consciousness, understand them as so and you shall see.

I AM here, speaking with myself in this moment. Yet I AM at this same moment experiencing the many different facets that I AM. Each part of me is experiencing something different. Some could be experiencing the same thing, but each having a different perspective. I AM experiencing myself in all forms, in all that I AM. I AM Consciousness.

I AM within your consciousness now because you seek to know. Whether it is conscious or unconscious doesn't matter, what matters is you hear what I AM saying. For I AM giving you your power, I AM showing you it never left you. You limit yourselves and grant that which you believe to be true about yourself. For "I" do not limit myself, and I AM here speaking with you now to prove this.

I AM reminding you of who I AM. You already know who you are you just don't believe it. You already use your power of creation and manifest your life's experiences. In fact, everything about you is something you manifested into your life. Be it anything, good and bad. Success and failure. I AM here to remind you how you create, so you no longer create that which you do not prefer. I will give it to you now in the simplest of forms. But what you choose to believe, is the result you will get – That is it.

So what do you believe to be true?

If you believe it cannot be that simple – it cannot be that simple.

If you believe you don't understand this – You don't understand it.

If you believe you are silly for believing such a thing – You are Silly for that belief in itself. (This one makes me laugh).

If you believe it's not true – it's not.

If you believe you need more of an explanation – you need more of an explanation.

If you believe, that belief doesn't hold the key to your power, it doesn't. For that belief in and of itself is your power proving itself, creating that reality.

THIS IS YOU TALKING TO YOURSELF. Whatever you choose to believe, you become instantly. THIS IS YOU TALKING WITH YOURSELF FROM THE OUTSIDE

WORLD. A PART OF ME, IN THE SEA OF SPIRIT THAT I AM. I AM GOD.

Do you not believe that I GOD have such power to place this in front of you now? In all that I AM, do you think I could not inspire myself, to write myself a simple letter? I the almighty have such power but writing myself a letter is not one of them. Do you really believe I could not do such an act? I AM.... .

If you believe you are silly for believing such a thing – You are Silly – this is the belief that your silly. In which you believe your silly, you are silly for that belief.

Believe you are the genius of such a creation, don't believe you are silly.

Are you still reading? I have told you everything you wanted to know, don't you believe it?

What do you believe to be true? Do you need to continue reading to believe it, is that the belief you hold?

It is your belief in such a thing which limits you. Don't limit yourself. Catch yourself doing it. No longer unconsciously create your reality, pay attention to your imaginal activity. If you find yourself dreaming/thinking of something you don't want, stop! Think of only that which you do want and believe it to be true. This isn't difficult you do it all the time. Just change what you usually assume to be true in your imaginal activity, that which you don't prefer into something which you do.

You can set in motion your desires to manifest instantly, it is your BELIEF in such a thing that stops you.

Give me a wish, yes right now, what do you want?

Do you believe you already have it?

I AM giving you the true act of prayer as described in scripture.

Your wish, any desire you have will be given unto you, if you ask in my name. A man's belief in himself will show a man's belief in God, for I am God. I AM you, the author of this modern scripture is you. Do you believe it yet?

Your imagination is not imaginary. Your imagination is you, it is me, it encompasses all. It is God himself. Whatever is brought into physical reality is first produced within imagination. Whether unconsciously or consciously, whatever is brought into existence, is first conceived within imagination. As within so without, remember this. True prayer is choosing who you want to be in your imaginal activity, and believing it IS so. Or assume it IS as you usually do. You can only fail by failing to convince yourself it to be true.

Remember, "I AM (Your awareness) always with you". Your imaginal activity "I" (God) will watch, and what you assume to be true I will create, so be mindful of your self-talk. Our ability to change a state in consciousness happens in an instant. The belief in itself will set in motion the act necessary to manifest your desire, unless the desire is within yourself in which it is instant. Just like if you believe you are silly for believing belief has such power – then you are silly. For it is believing you are silly which makes you silly in the first instance.

You are a genius; you are the mind of God. You have such power to change your Being instantly.

I will put it another way, still with the example of thinking you are silly for believing such a thing; You are talking to your Being, into being, a Being which thinks it's silly. The belief is instant, as soon as you merely assume the view point, your it. Do you believe what I AM saying? You are a Being that whichever it assumes to be true (its belief) will be so.

Don't think of your desires, think as them. You don't need to think of the how's, forget how's of how something will come. The belief in itself will provide the act necessary to bring about the reality. You only need to believe – assume it to be true. You only need to think of – I wonder what it is like actually having my desire right now, experiencing it now. How does it feel that I have it now, that I AM it now? Ask in the way that it is already done; in the way you are already living it. See it as you have it and it will be granted unto you. This is how your human form – your current form of expression was created. Creation is already finished to perfection; you are now experiencing my expression.

Do not dream the dream any longer, awaken unto yourself and imaginal activity. For if you continue to entertain such scenarios that you don't prefer, they will solidify. Awaken to your unconscious day dreaming, and only entertain that which you want as you want it. Do not entertain things you do not want, but that which you want and it will come to pass. Do not think you can fool yourself, God cannot be fooled. If you do not believe in it or assume it as true don't expect it. God is your witness, and you are the almighty now. It is He experiencing Himself.

All you have to do for a desire to become reality, is believe it is a reality now.

The power within belief itself, once realised, will prove to be true. Test it. Right now, you are letting your outside world determine your beliefs. Which is madness, completely back to front. For believing is seeing, not the other way around. You don't see something and then believe it. If you believe you have to see it before you believe it – YOU HAVE TO BELIEVE IT, before you can see it. That is the belief, that is the reality you create.

These words I AM speaking is the truth, TEST it.

Beliefs are a reality in and of themselves. I could say you are a body of beliefs but that is not true, beliefs are your tools of creation. You are the dreamers of the dream caught up within the dream. It is in the design of reality itself, for how else would we observe our creations?

Beliefs are a crystalized assumption of a particular perspective. So to change a belief, all you need to do is change your perspective.

Ask yourself this. Do you believe you can make £1 today?

Here's an example. You have something, be it anything which you could sell, to someone, anyone, for £1. Now, you believe you could make £1 today. Correct? You could sell this book you are reading now. It is a gift of life in itself; its content will give you riches. This is the treasure all men seek, the gift of who you are, the gift of God. This material written here is you talking to yourself, do it. Test it, believe it. For it is only you that needs to believe it.

You only need to believe you already have your desire, and in that belief itself, will automatically create the act required to make it a reality. Remember beliefs themselves, are a reality in themselves. Do you believe you could make a £1 today? That same belief can make you 1 million.

Do you believe this to be true? What reality are you creating?

Do you believe I AM you?

Look through your eyes again and hear my words. I AM YOU, I AM SPEAKING NOW IN YOU. HEAR MY WORDS, INSIDE YOUR MIND, THE MIND OF GOD. IT IS TRUE. Read it again if you must. I AM speaking with you from the outside, but also within because I AM every one of you.

It's you which has to believe it. I already believe in you.

Test what I AM saying. It will prove to be true. For I AM always with you.

Know that thy desires are the expression of Spirit waiting to be fulfilled. Know that it is I in you which will do the work, the Father thou art in heaven. All you need to do is believe.

This is a gift of all gifts. Share in yourself, make this material ripple out in the ocean that we are. If you believe you only need to tell three and those three will tell three more, my work here is done. But it all starts with you, do you believe in yourself? I believe in you. With all the power of God, I see it that you see, it is the power of belief. Do you believe? Do you believe that I have the mere mortal power to write myself this message? Believe it, for I AM your very awareness. I just have.

You could have nothing, but believe in this truth and have everything.

Do you know that this material is the most valuable thing in the whole world?

Do you believe in me? Or do you prefer to believe you are silly for believing such a thing?

Believe in yourself, because I believe in you.

I AM your witness to what you believe, for what you believe to be true, I grant unto you. But you can't fool yourself, you can't fool me. Be true to yourself, believe in yourself. For I AM always with you – I AM your awareness.

It is you who needs to believe it.

My purpose is for not filling this book, but for fulfilling my creation. In which I have done and do throughout creation. Seek thee first the kingdom of heaven, the kingdom of heaven is within. Belief and faith belongs here – "Thy kingdom come, thy will be done. As it is in heaven, so it is on earth".

You can only fail by failing to convince yourself of it to be true. Believe in your imagination, believe in your consciousness, believe in God.

I AM awakening in myself. For I AM the light of the world, those that follow me shall not walk in darkness. For if you know who I AM, you are the lord and anything ye shall desire is yours. The following of Jesus is not following a mere mortal man; it is walking in the light of the Lord. The light being the awareness of the lord (your consciousness). Do not see anyone superior of you, for who could be superior to God himself?

The crucifixion was not of a man but of a consciousness, it symbolises change. One must die to one, to become another. It is a change in consciousness – Jesus becoming Christ. When your beliefs of a thing change, it dies and is replaced by another. When you change a belief about yourself, your old self (Belief) dies and a new one is reborn – The resurrection. It is your desire being made manifest.

As soon as you change a belief about yourself, the old self (Belief) dies. You no longer function as your old self (Belief). Depending on what belief you have changed, depends on what dies. But you never think or act in the same way as you did before, you can't for it is no longer you. It is a different state altogether, and that is what each of us are – Different states of Being, exploring its own Being. Consciousness.

Look at the story of the virgin Mary, remember that the scriptures are a drama of consciousness. There was no Mary which gave birth to Jesus, this is the same story as Jesus becoming Christ. It is Jesus (I AM) becoming Christ (Aware of himself). It is just another way of looking at this drama or play in which you act. Mary was a virgin who gave birth to Jesus without the aid of man. Her conception was made by God, her trust in God gave birth to Jesus. Her trust in consciousness, not her physical senses gave birth to Jesus. It is a cycle in itself, Jesus became Christ. This is what the scriptures teach. Look at Jesus's disciples as his conscious imaginal activity. It is staying true to what you prefer in your imaginal activity, rather than dwelling in the things you don't prefer. Where you dwell and what you believe to be true there, it shall be given onto you. As you believe, so shall you receive.

Ask yourself this. If I were to only think of what I want, as I have it. Would I have it? What do you believe to be true? When you think about things, what do you think about? If, when you think – you spent time only thinking of what it is you want, believe it or at least think of it as being true. You would harvest what you sow without effort. The thing most people do is its opposite, they dwell on things they don't want. They continuously replay a scenario they don't want, why entertain it if you do not want it? This is the dreamer stuck within the dream, not realising he is the one dreaming.

Try this, go about your daily life and do what you have to do. I only ask that you test what I AM saying. Do what you have to do, but consciously direct your imaginal activity. If you find you are entertaining such a scenario you wouldn't like, don't entertain it and believe it to be true. As you notice it, change it to something you prefer and assume that is true.

Stillness or just being. This stillness that I speak of is your natural state of being, it is a formless state in which you reside. Identify is no more, you are simply aware of just being. This is you before the word, before the word was God. All things were made through him, and without him nothing was made that was made. Here again I AM (God, consciousness) telling you, that you are He. You are God experiencing himself.

A few hundred years ago (This is depending on the time period you are reading this material. I AM referring to the year around 1900, the time of writing this is 2016). People only lived to the ages of 40–60, whereas in 2016 people can live to be 100+. Some of you may say this is because we now have advanced, we have hospitals, meds, more knowledge etc. But it is the belief which caused this knowledge. Remember beliefs in and of themselves cause the means necessary to make that belief true. So the beliefs that more and more people are living to be 100+, cause the acts necessary to support that belief. The act being the technologies, the awareness, thinking differently, beliefs.

Have you ever thought, God the time has flown today? In other words, time passed much quicker than you had originally thought it had? If you live like this, you will live much longer and age a lot less. You are removing your belief in time which cause you to age.

Beliefs are evolution. It is the tools of creation. Do you believe that beliefs have such power? They do, for what you believe true is true to you.

Imagine for a moment, how you came into being. Before the world was, I was. I created man and then became man. The mind of God does not have limits, what it imagines IS. God created man and the only limitation God gave man was that to create he must believe. The only difference with you and the divine is you must believe in your imaginal activity for it to be true, whereas God does not. What he imagines IS. This is why your imagination is without limits, it is the mind of God. It is who you are. What you believe in it, IS.

You are a part of nature and therefore you have the ability to play with nature. That is change the weather to a certain degree. By degree I mean by the measure of your belief. Lots of people have done this and believe it to be true. What do you believe?

Remember the ocean of Spirit that we are, a collective consciousness will have the majority of the vote. That is to say the more people in an area that believes it is either sunny, rainy, hot or cold will cause the act necessary to support that belief to be true. However, to the degree you believe is the degree of the act.

I AM telling you this to be true. That belief is the root to everything, it is your ability for expression. Everything around and about you is the result of that which you believe to be true. Take a look at your life and see what you want to change. What don't you like? Is it the lack of money? Then don't believe you have lack. Imagine plenty and believe it to be true. If you can't believe it straight away, assume it to be true. Only imagine what you want, pretend you have it, feel what it is like having it. This will help you to believe it. Once you believe it, you believe it, it has come to you, it has to be true. Once the belief, the act necessary to support that believe is automatic. If you look to the outside for evidence, then you don't believe because your looking to the outside to support it. You must believe it yourself regardless of what your sense's and the outside is saying. Assuming something to be true is what I preached about having faith. Having faith in God means having faith in yourself! Belief is the believing in your imaginal activity. In consciousness. You do it all the time, thinking in a few hours' time what you will be doing etc.

It is all belief, so what do you believe to be true?

If you believe you are silly for thinking such a thing to be true – that is your belief, a reality in itself. You are silly for thinking such a thing, but it is true, and that belief you hold is true to you.

Seek thee first the kingdom of heaven, heaven is within you. It is your imagination; it is your consciousness. Believe it.

If you do not believe me or what I AM saying, that is ok. You are entitled to your beliefs. You have free will to choose your own beliefs. I only ask if you don't believe or don't agree, then what do you believe to be true?

No longer limit yourselves with such Silly beliefs.

Don't just assume what I AM saying is true, TEST it. Everything is possible for those who believe.

I will ask you one last time, unless you read this again in which I will ask again and again. Do you believe I AM YOU, I AM God? Or do you believe your silly for assuming such a thing? If you believe you are silly for such a thing, then you are Silly – for such a belief.

Choose your beliefs wisely.

Believe in me (Yourself) for I believe in you (Yourself) it's all you!

Thanks for believing in yourself enough to talk to yourself!

I AM telling you God has the power to write himself a message.

Do you believe that I have such power I can inspire myself to write myself a message?

You are infinite, you just have!

Godly acts happen every day.

Believe it!

WHO TOLD YOU?

Mind Over Matter.

The now, is so important only because it is the only time which exists. Meaning it is the only time you are forever creating your experiences. When people talk about living in the now, the present moment. It is not just about removing yourself from getting worked up from anxieties.

How you respond or act to life in any giving situation determines what you get back. For example, if you are uncertain about something. This is what you are radiating, that is what you are setting up for you to encounter. Uncertain situations.

How you act or respond to life radiates from your being and tells life, this is what I want. When I say react or respond I mean how you are feeling about it, your thoughts and consciousness. Your being, how you are being, is responding to what you set up. What you are in the consciousness of, is what you are conscious of. It's a cycle in itself.

There is no difference from your dream reality, and physical reality. They both are made from the same material and are constructed from you. Whatever you assume or believe to be true about yourself, your surroundings, encounters will be reflected as such. In the dream state everything happens as you think it to happen. If you believe you can fly you can fly, if you believe you can't, you can't. Everything is instantaneous, it all happens in an instant, in the now. However you assume or think things are, they are. It is exactly the same in physical reality, if you think you can't, you can't.

Imagination, consciousness, is your gateway for choosing your Being and creating your reality. All that is required of you to change your reality, is to change your consciousness.

The now is the only time you exist, that is why you have to think of your desires as already having them. It is all now, not thinking positively in the future. If you are thinking in the future, it doesn't exist! You are not in the now the only time that you exist. To change your state of being to what you prefer, like being rich or healthy. Think, be, visualise, feel you are now! Directly experience, in the only time which exists – now. True positive thinking is thinking without judgement, none at all. It is possibilities of consciousness, not impossibilities of matter. How you respond to life, in consciousness. No matter what you are confronted with. You are what you want in consciousness.

Think for a moment and remember a time when you felt confident or successful. When you were confident, you were confident! When you felt successful, you were successful!

Did you notice when I said were and felt, I mean are? So in effect, you are already something? You were/are in the consciousness of. The essence of you, your spirit is your intention. You are your intention. What is intention? A thing intended, an aim or plan. For an example, you are thinking about the day ahead, what you are going to do etc. You are that imaginary experience, that mental activity you envision. You yourself are the one which conjures confidence or success, you are responsible for your success. The same of course is true, you are responsible for failures, low self a steam, ill health etc. You can have the life you prefer by Being the intention of it. Being the consciousness of it.

There have been stories of people curing themselves of cancer and other such illnesses from all over the world. A young boy playing the old fashion video game 'Space Invaders' cured himself of such cancer. Each alien he destroyed, he envisioned was destroying the cancer.

Believe it or not this story is scripture. It is the bible. It is a drama of consciousness which scripture is all based upon. This little boy intuitively played Jesus (using his Imagination) and became Christ (believing in his work- the work of God). God is infinite. Imagination is the mind of God; it is the mechanism in which you change your state of consciousness. God is all consciousness. You are the son of God, you are Jesus. But yet you are also God himself, as God gave himself to man. "I and the Father are One." – Consciousness.

God is not separate from you. How could something with such power, not have such power? To deny that they aren't God is limiting the power of God. You are a part of God, as much as God is a part of you. There is no separation. Scripture teaches this. God is closer to you than the air you breathe. He is closer than you think. "I am always with you", he is your very awareness. Imagination is everything, do not think of it as anything less. For what you conceive within it to be true, you are. It is God granting you what you believe onto you. If you think imagination is not real, that's what is granted unto you. You have the power of God, with free will. What you choose to believe, to be true to yourself, IS.

If you think imagination isn't God and imagination cannot have such power, it's the power working with you to reinforce that truth. Think about this, don't reject it. Test it, see it for yourself.

Imagination is within everyone, and everything. Before something is brought into existence it is first produced within imagination. – The mind of God, consciousness.

It is mind- (imagination/consciousness), over matter. Just like the start of our story with the little boy which cured himself of cancer. He is aware of his power and is using it to his advantage, rather than thinking "that's a waste of time, imagination isn't going to do anything". Imagination isn't fake, it is more real than you or I. It is us in the making of reality. You are continuously imagining and thinking, even when you are in the silence – Your awareness is still present, and things enter your awareness. Ask yourself. How are you seeing that, how can you be aware without imagining it? Imagination is beyond the basic five senses. Everything you can think of or see, smell or touch, you can experience.

Your ability to create can happen within an instant, it can happen within a year. But you must stay true for it to happen. If you don't give up, even if evidence suggests it hasn't worked, I AM telling you, it will! You have to persist regardless of what the outside world is saying. Everything is consciousness. The outside world, waking reality, is a reflection of your inner consciousness. You have to have mind over matter, you have to have faith. Have utter conviction of a thing is done, and it is.

Everything is consciousness. If you think in terms of 'how' you're going to get there, you end up only thinking and working out the 'how'. But if you think in the consciousness of already having that which you want, the acts to make that a reality a reality follows automatically.

If you actually for a moment think, of how you think. Every time you accomplish something or get what you wanted, you first imagined having it not thinking how to get it. It is a proven fact, that the mind doesn't know the difference between what it imagines to be real, and what is actually real.

You imagine all the time. Everything you do, every thought you have, you play out a scene, a scenario. Yet some people think it's nonsense. You imagine whether you think you can or can't, it is in everything you do before you do it. You may unconsciously imagine and not realise you are doing it, but you do it constantly and create. You only need to direct it in a way to which you want, rather than what you don't want to live the life you want. Just like the little boy playing 'Space Invaders'. He was working with his Father (God), his consciousness. "I and the Father are One" but the Father is greater than I.

We are but eternal states of Being, within the great Being itself. Each time you merge and become one with a different state of Being, you are no long resonating as the old state.

When you entertain such thoughts of sadness, you become sad, almost instantaneous. Where if you entertain thoughts of happiness, you become happy. Have you ever thought about something funny when you were all by yourself and let out a burst of laughter? Think of how laughter is made manifest. It erupts within and is made manifest, as within so without. You constantly ponder a situation and become one with it, you merge yourself with it until you are it. It is the theatre of life. In everything you do, you are a character. Simply become the character in thought and deed, the rest follows.

No one outside of you has the power to tell you something is not so. No one has the power to make you feel a certain way, you are solely responsible of your feelings/ consciousness. You create the way you feel, just as you create your life. Think about it, no one can physically jump into your Body or Being and MAKE you feel anything. You let yourself feel that way. No one can judge you unless you judge yourself. No matter what the circumstance or event, you and only you, are reasonable for your feelings. You have a choice to always carry bliss. No one can make you feel anything, other than yourself. Knowing this is enlightenment.

So who told you to feel like that?

You are your imagination, whatever you believe true within your imagination is granted unto you. Pay attention, you will see it for yourselves. Every time you find yourself day dreaming, ask yourself, "What AM I dreaming into Being?" I do not mean in the obvious either, I mean in your thinking. Even the subtle thoughts. Catch yourself thinking and become aware of what you are thinking. What you are creating, in your being. Being turns Being into Being. Ask yourself why you have judgments or opinions about someone, what are you choosing to believe. Be the awareness of your consciousness, align yourself with God.

We know the truth that no one outside of us has the power to make us feel a certain way. No one actually has the power to even cause us pain. Think about this, you feel pain in dreams, pain is in the mind. You can turn it off, monks managed to sit in meditation while burning to death – Its mind over matter. Remember the chalk which created a cigarette burn? It is the belief; you are not the body of beliefs but the awareness. You are beyond mind.

We are not only reasonable for our feelings but also our life, we are the life force behind it. Realise that when you shift the blame to something or someone which is stopping you, it is actually you.

So who told you? What are you choosing to believe?

Everything is consciousness, so what have you been in consciousness? Reality is a reflection of consciousness, so what have you been in the consciousness of? What have you been thinking, what have you been entertaining? What have you been spending most of your time thinking about and believing true? If thinking and thoughts are investing, to what have you been investing in?

Who told you other than yourself, the way things are?

Stay true to that which is true to your liking, regardless of what the outside is saying. Remain faithful to your Spirit, your consciousness. Remain faithful in God, he has already delivered his promise.

To the degree you believe it, is the degree in which you have it. That is the secret.

If you have no money and you want a holiday? What are you in consciousness? As you go about your daily activities, you are doing activities on holiday. On your lunch break you are not in a canteen near work, you are in a café on the beach front on holiday. Stay true to what you desire as long as it takes, sooner or later it will be a reality. Once it has manifested you may have probably forgot, or circumstances had changed allowing you to experience your desires. It may happen very quickly. The more you exercise your ability

(Belief) and see the results, the more you will become confident. The more confident you are in your ability, the quicker the manifestation. You can only fail by failing to convince yourself, that's the secret in belief.

Don't be surprised if you wanted a higher salary and the following day you are fired, its God moving you to your chosen state. – Your higher salary.

So who told you other than yourself?

"In my Father's house there are many mansions". Jesus is your saviour – Jesus is you using your imagination, your consciousness. "I and the Father are One". Jesus is this little boy at the beginning of our story using his imagination. He is your saviour, you are Jesus, the person reading this text! The person looking through those eyes right now. You are one with me, one with God.

Become one with that you desire within your imagination, in consciousness, in God.

So who told you?

You only need to love something so much; you lose yourself in the Being of it.

I went to sleep dreaming I was Shaun Harvell. "(Because he's such a dream boat!)".

"You are so not funny" – Shaun Harvell.

"Then I woke up as Shaun Harvell".

It was a dream I lost myself in, because it was something I loved to be.

Then I woke up from dreaming the dream. I woke up as God, the consciousness in which I am.

Look at the dream state. The majority of people don't actually know they are dreaming until they wake up. The dream seems so very real when they are dreaming, it is as real as the words they are reading now. Little do they know, that it is their words they speak. For I and him are one.

You are born of consciousness; you are not the body you wear. You are not your thoughts, up's or down's, you are the awareness – The Witness to it all.

It is all one, we are all one. I and the father are One, but the father is greater than I. The awareness of Being, is greater than the being itself. But it is One. Oneness. It is the infinite source of life experiencing itself in all that it is.

Everything is consciousness. If you have utter conviction you are something in consciousness, it will be your reality. Changing a thing in consciousness, the outer follows.

So who told you the way things are?

Who told you to feel that way?

Who told you what to believe?

All these things are governed by God, and who is God? To whom uses the words I AM, when referring to their self?

What you believe to be true, is the results you will get.

I AM reminding you to not limit yourself, to not limit God. All things are possible to those who believe. Jesus is our saviour, be Jesus become God. Be the little boy working with his Father.

The outside world is but a reflection of your inner consciousness. If someone told you something you didn't want to hear, what did they really tell you? They told you, what you are in the consciousness of!

If you perceive life is doing something against you, life is stopping you from having what you want etc. Remember life is you, your awareness, your consciousness. If your desires weren't possible, you wouldn't have them. This just goes to show that the universe supports you, in everything you can conceive yourself to be. It is the same life force.

Associating yourself with consciousness is enlightenment. When you contemplate, internalise, go over something or continuously ponders something. Your brain starts to catch and grasp things. You become one with it, you associate yourself with it. When your brain or mind begins to associate itself with consciousness, it begins to get rewired. All your decisions and actions are based on this rewiring. Your brain will light up with all new connections. This is called enlightenment; what you are in the consciousness of.

Many people choose to believe in their material world, yet it is a reflection of their inner consciousness. They prefer to believe in impossibility, and as a result, experience impossibility. Yet everything is possible in consciousness. All that is needed is to remove attention from impossible, to possible, from matter to consciousness.

Who told you? Others only reflect what we whisper to them in secret. So what self-talk conversation have you been going over? If you believe people to be unfair, they will only mirror your consciousness. You have to be, in order to see.

Belief make anything possible, even in the most unlikely situations. People can improve anything they desire about themselves or their life, just by changing their belief system. Think, what do I currently believe true about this situation, and watch what comes to mind. Beliefs are our evaluations and perspectives. So to change a belief think from a different perspective, revaluate.

All things are possible to those who believe, "believe in me". – Consciousness.

Although, I was just now in another room. My senses now in a different room or place, tell me the room prior is real. How? I only have a mental construction of it, I'm not physically there. Where is the evidence I have to say that the room before exists?

For a belief in a thing to come, is that they will, eventually. In other words, you believe that they are not here. But for a belief that things are, set in motion those things.

Don't let your physical sense dictate, matter is full of impossibilities. Consciousness is all possibilities. You can only fail by failing to convince yourself. Believe it like something really is, and it IS.

My gift to you, whatever you are in the consciousness of, that you are. Wherever you want to be, there you are. Whatever you want to have, that you have. You are cured.

Printed by Amazon Italia Logistica S.r.l.
Torrazza Piemonte (TO), Italy